NATURAL STRESS MANAGEMENT

DR MIRIAM KINAI

CONTENTS

Acknowledgments

I would like to express my sincere gratitude to everyone who contributed in one way or another to the development of this publication.

I would especially like to thank
http://www.zazzle.com/ChristianArtGifts for their photographs.

1

DIET THERAPY

Foods that can help you manage stress naturally include:

1

Spinach

 Spinach is rich in vitamin A which is vital for stress management because it is a potent antioxidant. When the body is under stress more free radicals are produced and these can damage the cells. Potent antioxidants like vitamin A are thus needed to protect the body from free radical cell damage.

Spinach is also a rich source of other nutrients which are useful for managing stress. These include omega 3 fatty acids, vitamin B1, vitamin B3, vitamin B6 or pyridoxine, folic acid or folate or vitamin B9.

Raw spinach is also rich in vitamin C which is used by the body to regulate the function of the adrenal glands which produces cortisol and other stress hormones. Vitamin C is also thought to decrease the physical and psychological effects of stress.

Cooked spinach is rich in vitamin E which has a vital role in stress management since it is a potent antioxidant and thus mops up the free radicals responsible for free radical cell damage. Spinach is rich in iron and magnesium.

***

2

Fish

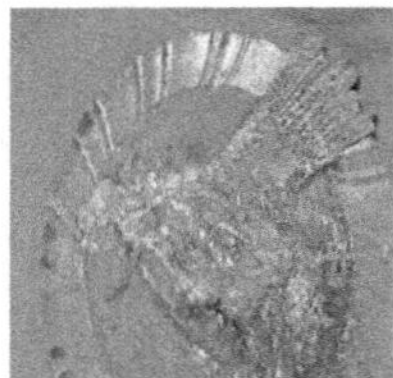

Fish are rich in omega 3 fatty acids which may help alleviate mood changes as well as control the level of stress hormones. Perfect examples include salmon, halibut, mackerel, tuna, anchovy, sardines, shad, and other fatty fish.

Fish is also a rich source of other nutrients which are useful for managing stress. These include tryptophan, vitamin B5 or pantothenic acid and selenium.

***

3

Sunflower Seeds

Sunflower seeds are rich in vitamin B1 or thiamine which is used by the body to convert dietary glucose into energy for physical activities and thus it may be beneficial for those with stress related lethargy.

Raw sunflower seeds are also rich in other stress management nutrients like omega 3 fatty acids, vitamin B6 or pyridoxine, folic acid or vitamin B9, vitamin E, magnesium and iron.

Sunflower seeds also contain selenium which is important for stress management since it is a potent antioxidant which reduces free radical cell damage.

***

4

Milk

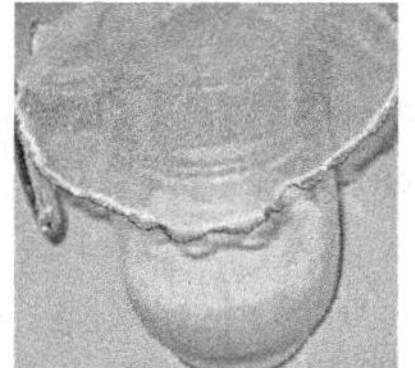

Milk raises the levels of serotonin which is a mood balancing hormone serotonin that also imparts a feeling of emotional well being.

Milk is a good source of calcium which makes it is effective for dealing with stress related insomnia or sleeplessness since calcium reduces tension by reducing muscle spasm and reducing anxiety.

Milk also contains phenylalanine which has been shown to enhance the production of dopamine by the brain.

Other stress management nutrients that can be obtained from milk include vitamin A, vitamin B2 or riboflavin, vitamin B12 or cyanocobalamin, selenium and magnesium.

***

5

Beef

Beef is rich in vitamin B3 or niacin which is used by the body to synthesize or make serotonin which is imparts a feeling of psychological well being.

Beef also contains tryptophan which is an amino acid that is vital for increasing the levels of serotonin, dopamine, and norepinephrine in the brain which help a person feel calm and alert.

Other stress management nutrients that are found in beef include vitamin B1 or thiamine, vitamin B5 or pantothenic acid, vitamin B6, vitamin B9 or folate, vitamin B12 or cyanocobalamin and selenium.

***

6

Oatmeal

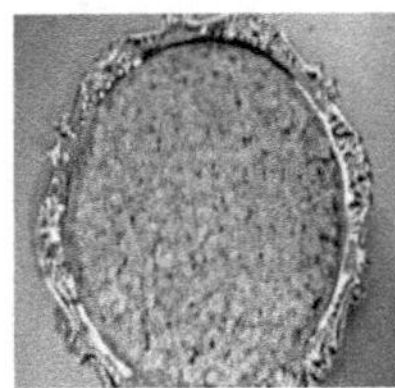

Oats are rich in vitamin B9 or folate which is used by the body to regulate the function of the adrenal glands which produce the stress hormones. It is thus vital for persons dealing with chronic stress. It is also important for those dealing with stress related depression since it is beneficial for managing depression.

Oatmeal increases the levels of serotonin which imparts a calm feeling of emotional well being.

Other stress management nutrients that are found in oatmeal include vitamin B1 or thiamine, vitamin B3 or niacin, selenium and magnesium.

***

7

Chicken

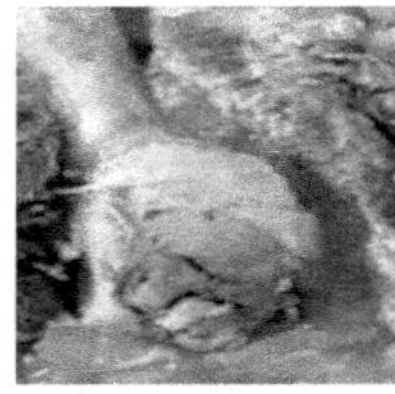

Chicken is rich in vitamin B6 or pyridoxine which is used by the body to synthesize serotonin which imparts a feeling of psychological well being. Low levels of serotonin are associated with depression which may be aggravated if it was already present due to the stressful situation.

Other stress management nutrients that are found in chicken include vitamin B3 or niacin, vitamin B5 or pantothenic acid and selenium.

Chicken contains stress management amino acids like tryptophan and tyrosine. Tryptophan is vital for increasing the levels of serotonin, dopamine, and norepinephrine in the brain which help a person feel calm and alert.

***

8

Liver

Liver is rich in iron which is important for managing stress since iron deficiency anemia is associated with symptoms of fatigue and apathy which may also be present as a result of the stress and thus become aggravated if the stressed person becomes anemic.

Other stress management nutrients found in liver include vitamin A, vitamin B3, vitamin B6, vitamin B9 and vitamin B12.

***

9

Whole Grain Bread

Whole grain bread is a complex carbohydrate which increases the levels of serotonin in the body. This serotonin "soothes the mind" and imparts a feeling of calmness, relaxation and emotional well being. These raised serotonin levels can also help a person with stress related sleeplessness sleep better.

Other stress management nutrients found in whole grain bread include folic acid, selenium, magnesium and tryptophan.

***

10

Eggs

Eggs contain tryptophan which is an amino acid that is vital for increasing the levels of serotonin, dopamine, and norepinephrine in the brain which help a person feel calm and alert.

Other stress management nutrients found in eggs include vitamin A, vitamin B12, selenium and tyrosine.

11

Broccoli

Broccoli is rich in vitamin C which is vital for managing stress since one study found that the blood pressures and levels of cortisol in people who took 3000 mg of Vitamin C before a stressful task reverted to normal levels more quickly.

Other stress management nutrients found in broccoli include omega 3 fatty acids, vitamin B3, vitamin B5 or pantothenic acid and iron.

12

Brown Rice

Brown rice is rich in selenium which is important for stress management since it is a potent antioxidant which reduces the free radical cell damage.

Brown rice also raises serotonin levels and imparts a feeling of calmness and emotional well being.

Other stress management nutrients that are found in brown rice include vitamin, vitamin B6 or pyridoxine and vitamin B9 or folic acid.

13

Beans

Beans, and especially the African Griffonia bean, are rich in tryptophan which is an amino acid that is vital for increasing the levels of serotonin, dopamine, and norepinephrine in the brain which helps you feel calm and more alert.

Other stress management nutrients that are found in beans include vitamin B1, vitamin B5, vitamin B9 or folic acid and selenium.

14

Yogurt

Yogurt contains vitamin B5 or pantothenic acid which is used by the body to regulate the function of the adrenal glands which release stress hormones such as adrenaline. It is therefore a vital nutrient for persons dealing with chronic stress.

Other stress management nutrients that are found in yogurt include vitamin B2 or riboflavin, vitamin B12 or cyanocobalamin and selenium.

****

15

Peanuts

Peanuts are rich in magnesium which is important for stress management since low magnesium levels can result in fatigue and headaches thus aggravate these symptoms if they are already present due to the stressful situation.

Peanuts are also very rich in vitamin E which has a vital role in stress management since it is a potent antioxidant and thus mops up the free radicals responsible for free radical cell damage.

Other stress management nutrients that are found in peanuts include vitamin B3 or niacin and folic acid or vitamin B9.

****

16

Soybeans And Soybean Oil

Soybeans and soybean oil are rich in omega 3 fatty acids which helps alleviate mood changes as well as control the level of stress hormones.

Dry roasted soybeans and soy bean sprouts are rich in folic acid or vitamin B9 which is used by the body to regulate the function of the adrenal glands which produce the stress hormones. It is thus vital for persons dealing with chronic stress.

Dry roasted soybeans are rich in magnesium which is important for stress management since low magnesium levels can result in fatigue and headaches thus aggravate these symptoms if they are already present due to the stressful situation.

Soy products also contain tyrosine.

****

17

Chocolate

Dark chocolate raises serotonin levels and thereby helps impart a feeling of emotional well being. In addition to its mood elevating properties, the simple act of eating chocolate, and other foods, endorphin levels which are the body's feel good hormones.

A Swiss study also found that people who ate 1.4 ounces (around 45 grams) of dark chocolate every day for a fortnight, had lower levels of cortisol and other stress hormones. This reduction was attributed to antioxidants called flavonoids in dark chocolate.

In addition, dark chocolate with at least 75% cocoa, reduces blood pressure, lowers levels of the bad LDL cholesterol, protects the body from free radical damage and provides it with iron. Other stress nutrients found in chocolate include magnesium and iron.

****

18

Avocados

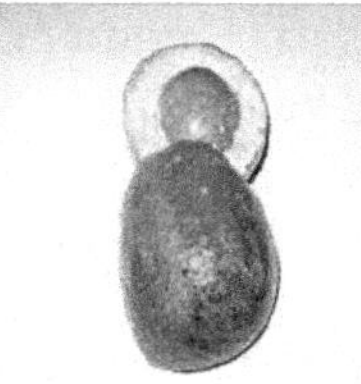

Avocados are rich in vitamin B3 or niacin which is used by the body to synthesize or make serotonin which is imparts a feeling of psychological well being.

Other stress management nutrients found in avocados include vitamin B5 and tyrosine.

***

19

Tea

Green tea leaves contain an amino acid known as L-theanine stimulates alpha brain waves and causes a calming effect on the body.

Green tea is also known to reduce feelings of anxiety. This is beneficial for stress related anxiety.

A study done on black tea revealed that it reduced levels of the stress hormone cortisol and resulted in the participants who drank it experiencing a greater sense of relaxation.

***

20

Bran

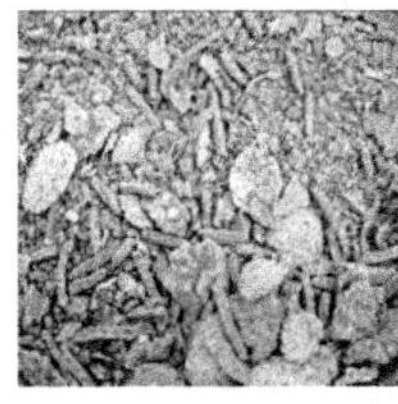

Rice and wheat bran are rich in vitamin B3 which is used by the body to synthesize or make serotonin which is imparts a feeling of psychological well being.

Other stress vitamins found in bran include vitamin B6 and magnesium.

***

21

Cheese

Cheese contains vitamin B12 which is beneficial for stress management since its deficiency is associated with irritability and mood swings which may also be present due to the stressful situation and thus worsen. Studies also suggest that vitamin B12 may ease mood changes.

Other stress management nutrients that are found in cheese include selenium and tryptophan.

***

22

Seaweed

Fresh seaweed is rich in omega 3 fatty acids which may help alleviate mood changes as well as control the level of stress hormones. Sea weed is also rich in iron.

***

23

Yeast Extract Spread

Yeast extract spread is rich in Vitamin B1. Raising B1 levels can result in an improved mood. Other stress nutrients found in yeast extract spread include vitamin B3 and folate.

* * * * *

2

SUPPLEMENTS

Supplements that are vital for supporting the body when it is dealing with the different biochemical processes that take place within it when it is dealing with a stressful situation include:

1.

Vitamin A

Vitamin A is a vital vitamin for stress management because it is a potent antioxidant. When the body is under stress more free radicals are produced and these can damage the cells. As a result, a potent antioxidant such as vitamin A is needed to mop up these free radicals and protect the body from free radical damage.

Therefore, if one is in a long standing stressful situation, they may need to take a vitamin A supplement if their dietary intake is inadequate.

Dietary sources of vitamin A include mangoes, carrots, sweet potatoes, papayas, red bell peppers, cantaloupes, milk, butter, eggs.

2.

B Complex Vitamins

There are several vitamin Bs which make up the B complex group of vitamins. These natural stress relief vitamins help in maintaining the proper functioning of the nervous system and are thought to help in reducing feelings of fatigue and sadness.

Since these B complex vitamins complement each other, they should be taken as combinations and not singularly.

Members of the B complex group of vitamins that are useful for the management of stress include:

Vitamin B1 or Thiamine

Thiamine is important for the management of stress since studies have shown that increasing thiamine levels in the body can result in improved moods.

Thiamine is also used by the body to convert dietary glucose into energy for physical activities and thus it may be beneficial for those with stress related lethargy.

Therefore, patients whose stress symptoms include feeling sad, depressed or fatigued may benefit from a thiamine supplement if they have inadequate dietary thiamine.

Dietary sources of thiamine include beans, meat, whole grain bread, cereals and nuts.

Vitamin B2 or Riboflavin

Riboflavin is used by the body to produce energy. Supplements may be beneficial to stressed, listless persons without adequate diet intake.

Dietary sources include milk, yogurt and dark green leafy vegetables.

Vitamin B3 or Niacin

Vitamin B3 or niacin is used by the body to synthesize serotonin which imparts a feeling of psychological well being. Low levels of serotonin are associated with depression which may be aggravated if it is already present due to the stressful situation.

Therefore, niacin supplements are useful for stressed patients who do not get enough niacin from their diet. Dietary sources of niacin include kidney, beef, whole grain cereals, liver, fish, avocados and dates.

****

Vitamin B5 or Pantothenic Acid

Pantothenic acid is used by the body to regulate the function of the adrenal glands which release stress hormones like adrenaline. Therefore, pantothenic acid acid supplements are important for chronic stress management by persons with inadequate dietary intake.

Dietary sources of pantothenic acid include beans, chicken, avocados, peas, beef, fish, broccoli, yogurt and sweet potatoes.

****

Vitamin B6 or Pyridoxine

Pyridoxine is used by the body to synthesize serotonin which imparts a feeling of psychological well being. Low levels of serotonin are associated with depression which may be aggravated if already present due to the stressful situation.

Pyridoxine is also important for the synthesis of melatonin which is important for maintaining the sleep wake cycle and thus vital for those experiencing stress related insomnia.

Therefore stressed persons not getting enough niacin from their diet should consider taking B complex supplements with pyridoxine. Dietary sources of pyridoxine include beef, whole grain cereals, dark green vegetables like spinach, brown rice, bananas

****

Vitamin B9 or Folic Acid

Folic acid is used by the body to regulate the function of the adrenal glands which produce the stress hormones. Vitamin B9 is also important for those with stress related depression since it is used for managing depression.

Therefore, a person undergoing chronic stress may benefit from folic acid supplements if they have inadequate dietary intake. Dietary sources include spinach, lettuce, beans, lemons, bananas, beef, liver and kidney.

Vitamin B12 or Cyanocobalamin

Cyanocobalamin deficiency is associated with irritability and mood swings which may also be present as a result of the stressful situation and thus worsen. Studies also suggest that it may ease mood changes.

Therefore, a person whose stress symptoms include feeling blue and moody may benefit from vitamin B12 supplements if they have inadequate dietary intake.

Dietary sources include milk, eggs, beef, fortified cereals and sea food.

3.

Vitamin E

Vitamin E is a potent antioxidant that mops up the free radicals and thus protects the body from free radical cell damage.

Therefore, a vitamin E supplement may benefit a stressed person not getting enough vitamin E from their diet.

Dietary sources of vitamin E include green leafy vegetables, peanuts, almonds and other nuts, eggs, avocados, sunflower seeds, sunflower oil, olive oil, maize oil and other oils.

4.

Vitamin C

Vitamin C is used by the body to regulate the function of the adrenal glands which produce cortisol and other stress hormones.

Vitamin C is also thought to decrease the physical and psychological effects of stress. One study found that the blood pressures and levels of cortisol in people who took 3000 mg of Vitamin C before a stressful task reverted to normal levels more quickly.

Vitamin C is also vital for stress management since it is a potent antioxidant and therefore reduces free radical cell damage. It also boosts the immune system function during stressful periods.

Therefore vitamin C is one of the most important supplements that a person experiencing chronic stress can take since it seems that vitamin C levels are depleted during chronic stress.

Dietary sources of vitamin C include oranges, grapefruit, tangerines and other citrus fruits, strawberries, cranberries, gooseberries and other berries, spinach, kale, mustard greens, cabbages and other green vegetables as well as tomatoes, green or red peppers, broccoli and papaya, pineapple and kiwifruit.

Since vitamin C is destroyed by cooking, eating raw fruits and vegetables is the best way to ensure adequate dietary intake.

****

5.

Calcium

Calcium is effective for dealing with the stress of sleep problems since it reduces tension by reducing muscle spasm and reducing anxiety.

Dietary sources of calcium include milk, cheese and other dairy products as well as almonds, sardines, salmon and spinach.

****

6.

Iron

Iron is important for managing stress since symptoms of iron deficiency anemia include fatigue and apathy which may also be present due to the stressful situation and thus become aggravated.

Women are more prone to developing iron deficiency anemia due to the loss of blood during menstruation. They should take iron supplements if tests confirms that they have iron deficiency anemia.

Dietary sources of iron include dark green leafy vegetables like spinach and kale, organ meats like liver as well as iron fortified cereals. Beans, seaweed and pure cocoa powder are other good sources.

7.

Magnesium

Magnesium is important for stress management since low levels of magnesium can result in fatigue and headaches thus aggravate these symptoms if they are already present due to the stressful situation.

Dietary sources of magnesium include green leafy vegetables like spinach, beans, broccoli, whole grain cereals and fish like salmon.

8.

Selenium

Selenium is vital since studies have linked a low intake with low moods. This may aggravate the low moods arising from the stressful situation. It is also protects the body from free radical cell damage.

Dietary sources of selenium include whole wheat bread, brown rice, fish, clams, oysters, chicken, pork, lamb, sunflower seeds, almonds, Brazil nuts, garlic, onions, eggs, beef and organ meats.

9.

Omega 3 Fatty Acids

Omega 3 fatty acid rich foods are vital for managing stress since they may help alleviate mood changes as well as control the level of stress hormones.

A study reported in the Archives of General Psychiatry revealed that taking 1 gram of fish oil daily decreased multiple symptoms such as suicidal ideation (thoughts of committing suicide), feelings of sadness, low libido, sleep problems, and anxiety by 50 percent. These symptoms were associated with depression but they can also be present in stressed patients.

Omega 3 fatty acids can lower high blood pressure and relieve the joint pains of arthritis both being conditions that are aggravated by stress.

Omega 3 fatty acids also have anti-inflammatory effects which can be useful for managing conditions like inflammatory bowel disease which is also aggravated by stress.

Omega 3 fatty acids can also reduce cholesterol and triglyceride levels.

Good dietary sources include oily fish like salmon, halibut, mackerel, tuna, anchovies, sardines and shad.

Flax seeds are also good sources of omega 3 fatty acids. You can grind two tablespoons of flax seeds each day and add them to you cereal, yogurt and salads.

Other good sources of omega 3 fatty acids include avocados, soybeans and soybean oil, walnuts, raw sunflower seeds, pumpkin seeds and chia seeds, spinach, broccoli as well as vegetable oils like canola and olive oil.

***

10.

Phenylalanine

Phenylalanine is an amino acid which has been shown to enhance the production of dopamine by the brain. Dietary sources of phenylalanine include milk.

***

11.

Tryptophan

Tryptophan is an amino acid which is vital for increasing the levels of serotonin, dopamine, and norepinephrine in the brain which help one feel calm and more alert. Dietary sources of tryptophan include fish, beef, eggs, beans, cheese.

***

12.

Tyrosine

Tyrosine is an amino acid and some studies suggest that when a person is stressed, their bodies are not able to produce enough tyrosine from another amino acid called phenylalanine. Studies also suggest that L-tyrosine supplements can help prevent memory and other cognitive decline in a person under physical stress like cold stress and extended wakefulness. Since more studies are needed, it does not harm to increase your dietary intake of tyrosine. Dietary sources of tryptophan include chicken, chicken, eggs.

* * * * *

3

HERBS

Herbs and spices that are useful for the management of stress include:

1

Chamomile

Chamomile has mentally relaxing properties and it is thus used to manage stress. It has been used for years as a relaxing tea which is typically taken after dinner since it also aids digestion and helps a person sleep better.

Its anti-inflammatory properties protect the body from free radical cell damage during stressful periods when more free radical are produced.

Chamomile also has sedative properties and it is used to manage insomnia.

Chamomile is used to relieve anxiety.

Do not use/ avoid chamomile if you are allergic to it or allergic to daisy or aster family plants such as ragweed and chrysanthemums.

Do not use/ avoid chamomile if you have asthma or are pregnant as it may cause miscarriage or you are driving as it may cause drowsiness or you are taking alcohol.

Do not use/avoid chamomile if you are scheduled to have surgery or dental procedures within 2 weeks as it may cause bleeding

***

2

Lemon Balm

Lemon balm has relaxing properties and it is thus used to manage stress. It is also able to uplift the emotions. It is also used to treat insomnia.

Its calming properties are useful for reliving anxiety.

Avoid lemon balm if you have hypothyroidism or low thyroid function.

***

3

Lavender

Lavender has scientifically proven mentally relaxing properties and it is therefore used for stress management. It is also used for managing stress related symptoms like indigestion, nervous exhaustion and tension headaches.

Lavender has sedative properties which are useful for treating sleeplessness.

Lavender has calming effects and it is used to relieve anxiety.

Do not use/ avoid lavender if you are pregnant or breastfeeding

***

4

Damiana

Damiana is used for mental relaxation.

Avoid it if you are pregnant or have diarrhea since it has a mild laxative effect.

5

Linden

Linden flowers are used to manage stress. They are also used for stress related ailments like tension headaches, anxiety and insomnia.

***

6

Passion Flower

Passionflower is used for stress management since ti helps reduce nervous tension.

It is also used to treat other stress related symptoms like anxiety, nervous tension and tension headaches.

Passionflower contains antioxidants and anti-inflammatory properties which protect the body from free radical cell damage which are produced in large amounts during stressful periods.

***

7

Bacopa

Bacopa is used to manage stress, anxiety and stress related memory problems. Avoid bacopa is you are taking anti-cholinergic medications or have a thyroid problem.

8

St. John's Wort

St John's wort's has been proven effective for the treatment of mild depression and it is also used to provide natural stress relief.

1. Do not use/ avoid St John's wort if you are allergic to it, have major or severe depression and bipolar disorder, are pregnant, breastfeeding or trying to get pregnant.

2. Do not expose the skin to sunlight after applying products containing St John's wort since it can make the skin photosensitive and thus more like to develop sunburns.

9

Skullcap

Skull cap helps the muscles relax. This is important since stress causes increased skeletal muscle tension.

Skullcap's calming properties are also useful for managing stress management and relieving anxiety, nervousness and restlessness.

The whole plant can be used to make a tea which is quite bitter therefore consider taking the tincture instead.

****

10

Kava Kava

Kava kava is a very effective muscle relaxer which also has calming properties that are useful for stress management. It is also used to relieve other stress related symptoms like restlessness, anxiety and insomnia or sleeplessness.

Do not take kava kava if you have liver disease or jaundice. Avoid it if driving or operating machinery or drinking alcohol heavily.

11

Licorice

Licorice root is thought to work as an adrenal tonic since it contains substances that boost adrenal gland function and help the body deal with stressful situations. It is therefore used for stress management.

****

12

Valerian

Valerian has relaxing properties which are useful for managing stress.

It makes a bitter tea, therefore consider mixing it with other more palatable herbs like lavender.

Do not use if you are using sedatives or medicines to help you sleep.

****

13

Holy Basil

Basil can act a natural tranquilizer by calming the nervous system and thus aiding in stress management. Its' powerful antioxidant are useful in protecting the body from free radical cell damage.

****

14

Ginseng

Panax ginseng roots are used for managing stress since they help establish a sense of calmness and emotional wellbeing.

Ginseng also helps improve energy levels and is used for nervous exhaustion. It also reduces feelings of sadness.

15

Chili Peppers

 Cayenne pepper or chili peppers are rich in Vitamin A which is vital vitamin for stress management because it is a potent antioxidant. When the body is under stress more free radicals are produced and these can damage the cells. As a result, a potent antioxidant such as vitamin A is needed to mop up these free radicals and protect the body from free radical damage.

Other stress management nutrients that are found in chili pepper and powder include vitamin B6 or pyridoxine, vitamin C and vitamin E.

***

16

Rhodiola

Rhodiola is also known as the golden root. It is used to relieve fatigue and manage stress and depression.

***

17

Lemon Verbana

Lemon verbena (Aloysia triphylla) leaves and stems are used to relieve insomnia or sleeplessness.

***

18

Catnip

Catnip is used to treat insomnia and nervous indigestion.

***

19

Tea

Green tea leaves contain an amino acid known as L-theanine which has been found to stimulate alpha brain waves and this results in a calming effect on the body.

Green tea is also known to reduce feelings of anxiety. This is especially beneficial for persons dealing with stress who are also anxious.

A study done on black tea revealed that it reduced levels of the stress hormone cortisol and resulted in the participants who drank it experiencing a greater sense of relaxation.

* * * * *

4

ESSENTIAL OILS

Essential oils that are used for managing stress include:

Ylang Ylang Essential Oil

Name: Cananga odorata

Method of Extraction: Steam distilled from flowers

Perfumery Note: Base note

Strength of Initial Aroma: Strong

Aromatic Description: Fragrantly floral

Ylang Ylang Essential Oil Safety Information

1. Avoid it if you have low blood pressure.

2. Avoid using it if you have sensitive or damaged skin.

3. Avoid using more than 1% concentrations since high concentrations can cause headaches and nausea.

Clary Sage Essential Oil

Name: Salvia sclarea

Method of Extraction: Steam distilled from the flowering tops

Color: Golden to yellow

Perfumery Note: Top note

Odor Intensity: 5

Strength of Initial Aroma: Medium

Aromatic Description: Herbaceous

Characteristics: Nontoxic and non-irritant.

**

Clary Sage Essential Oil Safety Information

1. Do not use it during pregnancy.

2. Do not use it if you are drinking alcohol or driving.

3. Do not use if if you have endometriosis, ovarian cysts, uterine cysts, breast cancer or you are at high risk for developing breast cancer as it may have an "estrogen-like" effect on the body.

4. Preparations with a high concentration of clary sage can result in a narcotic effect. Therefore, avoid using more than 0.8% concentrations.

5. Clary sage can also cause headaches.

6. Do not use it alone for more than 2-3 months as it may lead to sensitization.

***

Lavender Essential Oil

Name: Lavendula officinalis

Method of Extraction: Steam distilled from the flowers

Color: Clear to yellow

Perfumery Note: Middle note

Odor Intensity: 4

Strength of Initial Aroma: Medium

Aromatic Description: Sweet, soothing, floral and fruity

Characteristics: Nontoxic, non-irritant and non-sensitizing. Can be used on all skin types

**

Lavender Essential Oil Safety Information

1. Do not use it in pregnancy especially the first 3 months.

2. Do not use it if you are breastfeeding.

3. Do not use it on young children as it may cause breast development in boys (gynaecomastia) and girls (pre-pubescent breast development).

4. Avoid it if you have low blood pressure as you may feel drowsy after using it.

5. Do not use it alone for more than 2-3 months as it may lead to sensitization.

***

Natural Stress Management Essential Oil Recipes

The first step in using essential oils is to do a patch test for each of the essential oils that you want to use.

To do this, apply the essential oil that has been diluted with a carrier oil on the inner aspect of your elbow, bandage it and wait for 24 hours to see if you will develop rashes or itchiness or swelling or any other sign of an allergic reaction. If you do, do not use that essential oil.

The second step is to create the stress management essential oil blend. You can create a simple one by mixing 10 drops of Ylang ylang essential oil, 10 drops of rose essential oil, 20 drops of Lavender essential oil and 30 drops of Clary sage essential oil in a dark bottle. We will refer to this mixture as the "Relaxation Blend" in the recipes.

Therefore, if the recipe says, "Add 12 drops of the Relaxation Blend", you simply add 12 drops of this mixture of essential oils.

If you just want to buy one aromatherapy oil, I would recommend lavender essential oil. Likewise, if the recipe says, "Add 12 drops of the Relaxation Blend", you simply add 12 drops of lavender essential oil.

***

Aromatherapy Bath.

Create a relaxing bath by dispersing 12 drops of the "Relaxation Blend" in your warm bath water. You can also mix it with milk to help it disperse.

Bath Gel.

Add 50 drops (2.5 ml or ½ teaspoons) of the "Relaxation Blend" to one cup (8 oz or 250 ml) of unscented bath gel or liquid soap to create a relaxing bath gel.

Body Brush. Add 2 drops of the "Relaxation Blend" to the natural bristles of a bath brush and brush your entire skin before bathing to stimulate it and get rid of the dead skin cells.

Bath Salts.

Mix 2 cups Epsom salts, 1 cup sea salt and 1 cup baking soda. Add 50 drops (2.5 ml) of the "Relaxation Blend" and a few drops of food coloring (optional). Add one cup of these bath salts to your warm bath water for a relaxing soak.

Bath Tea.

Mix 2 cups of herbs like lavender flowers and rosemary leaves, drops of the "Relaxation Blend" and 1 cup of sea salt. Put them in an air tight jar or you can add a scoopful of the mixture into bath tea bag and store the filled bath tea bags in the air tight

Body Scrub.

Scrub the stress away by adding 50 drops (2.5 ml or ½ te
the "Relaxation Blend" to one cup (8 oz or 250 ml) of sw
oil or sunflower oil or any other carrier oil. Mix it with ½ c of
Epsom salts or brown sugar or white sugar. Rub if all over y
to remove the dead skin cells then rinse it off to reveal baby s

Body Wrap.

Add 20 drops of the "Relaxation Blend" to 3 oz or 100 ml of distilled
water and spray it on your towel. Wrap your body in the towel and
then wrap a plastic sheet around yourself and relax for 20 minutes
before you unwrap yourself.

Body

Add 5
one cup 5 ml or ½ teaspoons) of the "Relaxation Blend" to
other c 250 ml) of sweet almond oil or sunflower oil or any
your skin use it as an after shower body oil. Massage it into
moisture g it dry but while it is still moist to lock in the
benefits of lavender.

Aloe Vera Aromatherapy Gel.

Add 50 drops of the "Relaxation Blend" to one cup (8 oz or 250 ml) of natural aloe vera gel to create a non-greasy, healing moisturizer.

Body Massage Oil.

Add 50 drops (2.5 ml or ½ teaspoons) of the "Relaxation Blend" to one cup (8 oz or 250 ml) of sweet almond oil or sunflower oil or any other carrier oil to create a relaxing body massage oil.

Back Self Massager.

If you want to give yourself a self massage, simply apply the aromatherapy body massage oil with the "Relaxation Blend" to your back and then holding the handles of the back self massager, run the rollers to and fro across your back. This self massager can also be used for neck and leg self massages.

Mini Self Massage Oil.

Add 1 drop of the "Relaxation Blend" to 5 ml of sweet almond oil or any other carrier oil of your choice and put it in a small bottle that can fit into your purse to pocket. Carry it with you for 5 minute mini – self massages to massage your temples or the back of your neck whenever you begin to feel tense.

Personal perfume.

Put 10 ml jojoba in a bottle and add 60 drops of the "Relaxation Blend" followed by 10 ml of 99% alcohol isopropyl in a spray bottle to make your own stress relieving perfume.

Facial Steamer.

Add 50 drops of the "Relaxation Blend" (or the number or drops recommended by the manufacturer) to one cup (8oz or 250 ml) of water and put it on your facial steamer or sauna.

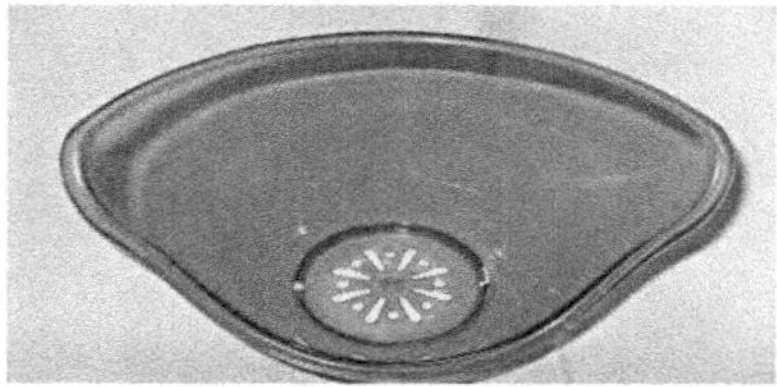

Scalp Massager.

Apply the aromatherapy hair oil with the "Relaxation Blend" to the scalp and then use the scalp massager to brush and distribute the healing oils from the roots to the ends.

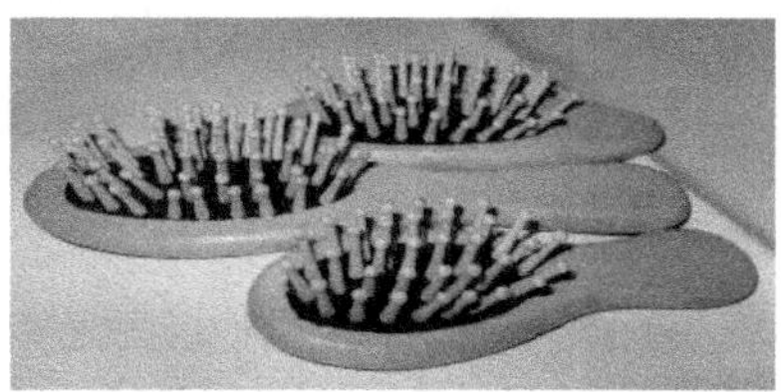

Head Massager.

Gently twirl the long fingers of the head massager to stimulate acupressure points on your scalp, increase circulation and reduce tension after applying the aromatherapy hair oil with the "Relaxation Blend".

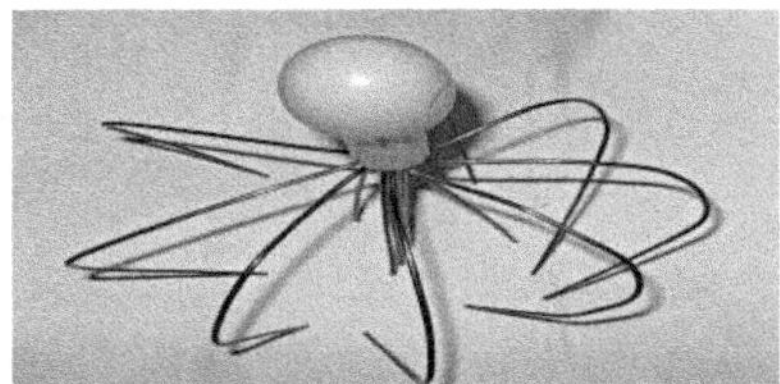

Foot Bath.

Create your own soothing foot bath blend by adding 12 drops of the "Relaxation Blend" to a bowl of warm water to soak your feet.

Foot Oil.

Add 6 drops of the "Relaxation Blend" to 30 ml of sweet almond oil or any other carrier oil of your choice. Use it to massage your feet after your foot bath and before you wrap them in soft cotton socks.

Foot Roller.

Give yourself a foot massage by applying an aromatherapy foot oil with the "Relaxation Blend" to your feet and then moving them to and fro on the foot roller. This will help ease tension and improve the circulation of blood in your feet and reduce some types of foot pain.

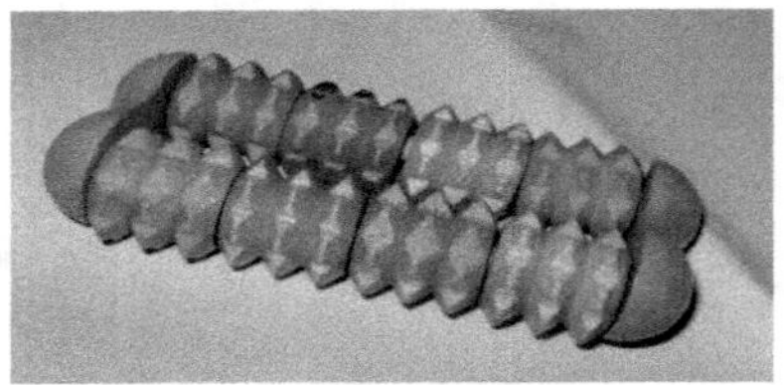

Petroleim Jelly Hand Cream.

Melt 2 teaspoons of a petroleum jelly such as Vaseline, add 6 drops of the "Relaxation Blend" when cool and then pour into a jar.

Linen Spray.

Add 250 drops (12.5 ml or 2.5 teaspoons) of the "Relaxation Blend" to one cup (8 oz or 250 ml) of distilled or plain water and use it as a linen spray to spritz your bed sheets.

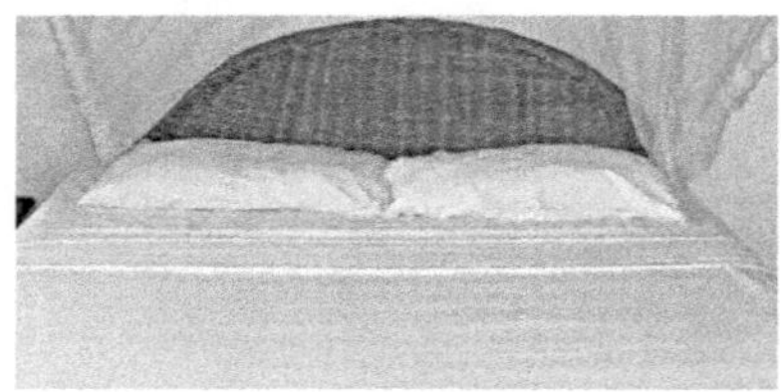

Scent Balls.

Add 6 drops of the "Relaxation Blend" to your handkerchief or a cotton ball or sponge and sniff it throughout the day whenever you begin to feel tense.

Room Fragrance.

Add 24 drops of the "Relaxation Blend" to your diffuser. If your diffuser comes with instructions, use the number of drops recommended by the manufacturer.

Room Scent.

Add 12 drops of the "Relaxation Blend" to ¼ cup (2 oz or 60 ml) of water, place it on an oil warmer and light the candle to scatter the soothing scent.

Light Bulb Scent.

Drop 3 drops of the "Relaxation Blend" to a light bulb when the light is switched off, switch it on to illuminate and scent your room.

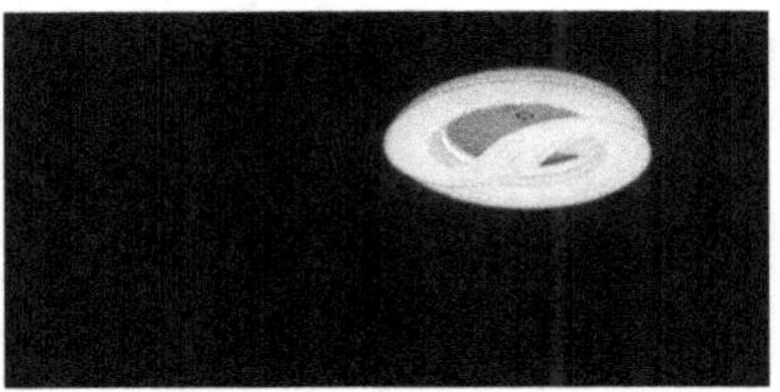

Aroma Ring Scent.

Add 5 drops of the "Relaxation Blend" to an aroma oil ring, place it on top of your lamp bulb, light the lamp and experience relaxing light.

Car Diffuser.

Add the "Relaxation Blend" to your car's diffuser according to the manufacturer's instructions and let the soothing scent envelope you as you drive.

* * * * *

5

LIFESTYLE MODIFICATIONS

Lifestyle modifications that can help you manage stress naturally include:

1.

Exercising Regularly

Stretching Exercises

Stretching your muscles helps manage stress since stress increases muscle tension while stretching reduces it and relaxes the muscles.

Therefore, stretch for at least 10 minutes every day and also during the warm up and cool down periods of exercising. When stretching, pay more attention to those muscles that you tense when you are stressed. These may be your neck, shoulder or back muscles. In addition, stretch these muscles whenever you notice that you are 'getting tense' so that you can release the tension.

Weight Bearing Exercises

Strength training or weight bearing exercises can help you relax since they demand total mental concentration and thus take your attention from all the events that maybe stressing you.

Therefore engage in weight bearing exercises as part of your stress management plan. As you do so, ensure that you do not strength train the same muscle group for two consecutive days. If you don't know how to strength train safely, join a gym and train under qualified supervision to get the basics correct.

Aerobic Exercises

Aerobic exercises reduce the levels of circulating stress hormones and thus decrease your chances of developing stress related illnesses. They also increase levels of endorphins which make a person feel good. Aerobic exercises also clear a person's mind and reduce tension.

Therefore, "work out" all the stress and tension from your body by regularly engaging in aerobic activities like brisk walking, jogging, running, dancing, swimming, playing basketball, rugby, football, housework, work or aerobic classes at your local gym.

2.

Spending Time in Nature

Periodically schedule time to get away from confining cubicles, austere computer screens, glaring artificial lights, nagging phones and polluted city air so that you can spend time in natural surroundings like forests and beaches.

Rest your eyes on the gentle greens and soothing blues as you listen to twittering birds, ocean waves and other nature sounds which are known to calm the mind.

3.

Steam Bathing

Saunas and steam baths are helpful for managing stress since they help relieve muscle tension. Therefore schedule at least 15 minutes each week to sweat away your stress in a hot room.

***

4.

Keeping Pets

Pets are very useful for reducing the impact of stress especially for people who live alone. They are able to do this since they offer companionship and provide something to care for that is nonjudgmental.

Pet ownership also confers other health benefits since studies have shown that people who own pets have significantly lower blood pressure than those who do not own any.

Therefore, if you are stressed and lonely, it may be well worth your while to get a pet and pet it regularly.

***

5.

Sleeping

Getting adequate sleep is another way of dealing with stress naturally since it rests the mind and rejuvenates the body. Therefore aim for 8 to 10 hours each night.

***

6.

Listening To Music

Medical research tells us that listening to soothing music can help a person relax.

The Bible confirms these findings because we can see that **Whenever the tormenting spirit troubled King Saul, David would play the harp and Saul would feel better. (1 Samuel 16:23)**

Therefore, since music has the power to relax tense minds, soothe troubled spirits and elevate depressed feelings, schedule time to listen to soothing instrumentals.

***

7.

Singing

Singing is known to reduce tension. Singing praises is even more effective because of the power that is latent in praising God for **He is Enthroned in the praises**. (Psalm 22:3). Therefore create time to sing and preferably sing Christian praise songs.

***

8.

Basking

Basking can help manage stress naturally since exposure to sunlight increases the levels of serotonin in the body. Serotonin is a mood lifting hormone which can impart a feeling of calmness, relaxation and emotional well being.

Therefore, apply sunscreen and schedule a few minutes to spend enjoying the sunlight especially if you are in the middle of a stressful situation.

***

9.

Pampering Yourself

Get in the habit of spoiling yourself at least once a week so that you can feel better and relax in the midst of a stressful situation.

You can check into a day spa or into your home spa. You can buy a new outfit or update an old one with new buttons. You can get a new hair cut at a posh salon or style your current one at home in a different way. You can eat out at a five star restaurant or prepare your own gourmet meal at home. You can treat yourself to a luxurious hot paraffin mani/pedi or give yourself a simple pedicure at home using natural products.

Since the options for pampering yourself vary depending on your financial situation and mental disposition, what matters is not what you do but that you do something that makes you feel good.

****

10.

Engaging In Complementary Hobbies

Engaging in hobbies that complement your day job or how you spend your 9-5 if you are unemployed is another way of relaxing in the middle of a stressful situation.

For example if you an accountant who spends their 9-5 confined in a cubicle with computers crunching up numbers, you can take up "people-based" hobby like playing golf or rugby or singing in a choir.

If you spend your 9-5 as a customer service representative responding to requests from unsatisfied clients, you can engage in a solitary hobby like writing or painting.

If you spend most of your waking hours with children as a stay at home mom or a teacher, you can choose an "adult-centered" hobby like discussing books in a book club to complement your 9-5.

****

11.

Getting a Massage

When a person is facing a stressful situation, their muscles become tense. By getting a massage which rubs and kneads the tense muscles until they relax, the person is able to feel relaxed.

Therefore create time to have a professional massage therapist work the tension out of all your muscles. Enhance the experience by using relaxing massage oils like those which contain lavender essential oil.

***

12.

Watching Comedy

Schedule at least 30 minutes every day to engage in hearty laughter since laughter is known relieve tension and reduce stress hormones.

6

EXERCISE PLAN

A balanced exercise plan should combine stretching, weight bearing and aerobic exercises.

If you have been leading a sedentary lifestyle, consult your doctor and nutritionist before making changes to your exercise regimen.

In addition, invest in a good pair of sports shoes that will cushion your feet and redistribute your weight evenly as you walk, jog, jump or run.

If as you exercise, you experience any of the following symptoms, stop exercising at once and consult your doctor: chest pain, pressure or tightness, unusual shortness of breath, pain in the jaw, arm, neck or shoulder, palpitations or skipped heart beats, feeling dizzy or fainting, muscle pain that is more severe than just discomfort.

1.

Stretching Exercises

Stretch for at least 10 minutes each morning and evening and in the warm up and cool down periods just before or right after your exercise sessions.

To stretch correctly you should:

1. Not hold your breath as you stretch. Breathe in and out rhythmically.

2. Never bounce into or out of your stretches. Gently move into and out of the various positions.

3. Hold the stretch position for 10 seconds and gradually increase the duration.

4. Be systematic and begin with the legs as you work your way up the body to the neck or vice versa.

5. Stop stretching if you feel any pain but continue if you experience mild discomfort.

The following is a list of exercises that you can do at home to stretch your entire body.

1. Neck Stretch - Stand with your feet shoulder width apart and your chin on your chest. Rotate your head once clockwise. Return chest to chin and rotate it counter clockwise. Do several rotations. Turn your face to the right, look as far back over your shoulder as you can. Hold for a count of 10. Repeat on opposite side.

2. Chest, Shoulder and Arm Stretch - Stand with your feet shoulder width apart and your knees slightly bent. Clasp your hands behind your back and push them back as far as you can reach. Push your chest forward as far as it can reach. Hold and return to starting position.

3. Side Stretch - Stand straight with your arms raised over your head. Tilt your body to the left side as you stretch your side muscles. Hold. Repeat on the opposite side.

4. Abs, Glutes and Quads Stretch - Stand with your feet together. Reach forward with your right arm. Lift your left leg behind you and grasp your left ankle with your left hand. Lift your left thigh as high as you can or until it is parallel to the ground. Repeat on opposite side.

5. Back Stretch - Lie on your back and pull both knees to your chest. Release them and lower your knees to the right side and then to the left side. Return knees back to chest.

6. Hamstring Stretch - Lie on your back with your legs bent and both feet flat on the floor. Straighten and raise your right leg. Gently pull your right thigh towards your body and hold for a count of 10. Repeat on the opposite side.

2.

Weight Bearing Exercises

To weight train or strength train correctly you should:

a) Not hold your breath or strain as you train.

b) Not exercise the same muscle groups for two consecutive days.

c) Aim for 3 sets of 10 repetitions each.

The following are exercises that you can do at home to strength train your entire body.

1. Overhead Press - (Works shoulders) Sit on a chair; hold a weight (or a full water bottle) in each hand at shoulder level with palms facing forward. Raise your arms straight up over your head. Lower them to shoulder level.

2. Biceps Curl - (Works biceps) Sit on a chair; hold a weight (or a full water bottle) in each hand palms facing forward. Bend your elbow and lift the weight towards your shoulder. Return to starting position and repeat with the other arm.

3. Triceps Dips - (Works triceps) Sit on the edge of a sturdy chair with your back and shoulders straight. Hold the edge of a chair and bend your elbows to form a right angle as you lower your butt off the seat to the floor. Straighten your arms and press back up to raise your butt back to the seat.

4. Push Ups - (Works deltoids, triceps, pectorals) Lie on floor, palms face down, elbows bent next to shoulders. Push up from floor by straightening elbows and contracting abs so that your body forms a straight line from your head to heel (beginners can rest both knees on floor) Lower yourself to floor by bending elbows. Push back up.

5. Simple Straight Crunches - (Works abs) Lie flat on your back; bend knees while keeping your feet flat on the floor. Place your hands on your thighs. Exhale and lift shoulder blades from the floor as you slide your hands up to your knees. Hold for a count of 10. Return to starting position and repeat.

6. Simple Side Crunches - (Works abs) Lie flat on your back; bend knees while keeping your feet flat on the floor. Place your hands on your right thigh. Exhale and lift shoulder blades from the floor as you slide your hands up to your right knee. Hold for a count of 10. Return to starting position and repeat. Do on opposite side.

7. Advanced Straight Crunches - (Works abs) Lie flat on your back; bend your knees until thighs are perpendicular to floor. Place arms crossed over your chest. Exhale, tighten abs and lift shoulder blades from the floor as you reach towards knees. Hold for a count of 10. Return to starting position and repeat.

8. Advanced Side Crunches - (Works abs) Lie flat on your back; bend your knees until thighs are perpendicular to floor. Place arms crossed over your chest. Exhale, tighten abs and lift shoulder blades from floor as you reach towards right knee. Hold for a count of 10. Return to starting position and repeat. Do on opposite side.

9. Leg Lifts - Lie on your back; legs straight; hands under butt. Lift legs 30 cm from the floor. Hold for a count of 10.

10. Lunge - (Works glutes, hamstrings, quadriceps) Stand with feet shoulder width apart, arms at sides. Take a large step forward with your left leg and ensure your left knee is above your left foot. Lower your body to the floor by bending the right knee until right thigh is parallel to the floor and right knee is close to the ground. Squeeze your glutes as you press back up to your starting position. Repeat on opposite side.

11. Squat - (Works your butt and thighs) Stand with your feet parallel and shoulder width apart. Stretch out your hands in front of you. Keeping your abs and butt tight, bend your knees and slowly lower yourself as though you are sitting. Ensure your knees don't extend past your toes. Hold for a count of 10. As your rise, squeeze your glutes.

12. Calf Raises - (Work your calf muscles) Stand with feet together and arms raised above your head. Lift your heels so that you are standing on the balls of your feet/toes. Stand on your toes for a count of 10.

***

3.

Aerobic Exercises

Aerobic exercises include walking, skipping a rope, jogging (on a treadmill or in the park), cycling or spinning in the gym, swimming, aerobic classes in a gym, sports like tennis and basketball as well as everyday activities like climbing stairs, housework and gardening.

Swimming is a good option especially if you are overweight or obese because it does not put excessive pressure on the joints of the lower limbs.

To reap the most benefits from your aerobic exercise sessions, you should:

1. Exercise for at least 30 min each session

2. Reach your Target Heart Rate (THR) which is calculated by

220 - your age = maximum heart rate (MHR)

MHR x 0.65 = minimum target heart rate (MinTHR)

MHR x 0.80 = maximum target heart rate (MaxTHR)

For example, if you are 40 years old, 220 - 40 years = 180 your maximum heart rate (MHR)

180 (MHR) x 0.65 = 117 your minimum target heart rate (MinTHR)

180 (MHR) x 0.80 = 144 your maximum target heart rate (MaxTHR)

Therefore, as you exercise, you should ensure that your heart rate is between 117 and 144.

To know your heart rate per minute, take your pulse on your wrist or neck for one minute.

The following is a rough guide of target heart rates for different age groups:

If you are 20 years old, your Target Heart Rate (THR) per minute should be 130 - 160

If you are 30 years old, your Target Heart Rate (THR) per minute should be 123 – 152

If you are 40 years old, your Target Heart Rate (THR) per minute should be 117 – 144

If you are 50 years old, your Target Heart Rate (THR) per minute should be 110 – 136

If you are 60 years old, your Target Heart Rate (THR) per minute should be 104 – 128

If you are 70 years old, your Target Heart Rate (THR) per minute should be 97 – 120

If you are 80 years old, your Target Heart Rate (THR) per minute should be 91 – 112

Exercise Plan

You can modify this plan to suit your lifestyle and level of activity.

Exercise Activity for Week 1

Day 1

Whole body stretch to warm up

30 min walk at minimum THR

Whole body stretch to cool down

Day 2

Whole body stretch to warm up

10 push ups, 10 triceps dips, 10 crunches

Whole body stretch to cool down

Day 3

Whole body stretch to warm up

30 min walk at minimum THR

Whole body stretch to cool down

Day 4

Whole body stretch to warm up

10 squats, 10 lunges, 10 calf raises, 10 crunches

Whole body stretch to cool down

Day 5

Whole body stretch to warm up

30 min walk at minimum THR

Whole body stretch to cool down

Exercise Activity for week 2

Day 1

Whole body stretch to warm up

30 min walk/ jog at medium THR

Whole body stretch to cool down

Day 2

Whole body stretch to warm up

15 push ups, 15 bicep curls, 15 triceps dips, 15 crunches

Whole body stretch to cool down

Day 3

Whole body stretch to warm up

30 min walk/ jog at medium THR

Whole body stretch to cool down

Day 4

Whole body stretch to warm up

15 squats, 15 lunges, 15 calf raises, 15 crunches

Whole body stretch to cool down

Day 5

Whole body stretch to warm up

30 min walk/ jog at medium THR

Whole body stretch to cool down

Exercise Activity for week 3

Day 1

Whole body stretch to warm up

30 min walk/run maximum THR

Whole body stretch to cool down

Day 2

Whole body stretch to warm up

20 push ups, 20 bicep curls, 20 triceps dips, 20 crunches

Whole body stretch to cool down

Day 3

Whole body stretch to warm up

30 min walk/run maximum THR

Whole body stretch to cool down

Day 4

Whole body stretch to warm up

20 squats, 20 lunges, 20 calf raises, 20 crunches

Whole body stretch to cool down

Day 5

Whole body stretch to warm up

30 min walk/run maximum THR

Whole body stretch to cool down

Exercise Activity for week 4

Day 1

Whole body stretch to warm up

30 min walk/run maximum THR

Whole body stretch to cool down

Day 2

Whole body stretch to warm up

30 push ups, 30 bicep curls, 30 triceps dips, 30 crunches

Whole body stretch to cool down

Day 3

Whole body stretch to warm up

30 min walk/run maximum THR

Whole body stretch to cool down

Day 4

Whole body stretch to warm up

30 push ups, 30 bicep curls, 30 triceps dips, 30 crunches

Whole body stretch to cool down

Day 5

Whole body stretch to warm up

30 min walk/run maximum THR

Whole body stretch to cool down

* * * * *

7

STRESS MANAGEMENT PLAN

Learning and practicing relaxation techniques is a very effective way of managing stress. These relaxation techniques include:

1.

Meditation

Meditation is another effective relaxation technique for coping with stress. To meditate, simply lie down in a quiet place and take several deep breaths. Once your body begins to feel calmer, focus on your inhalation and on the pure oxygen entering your body. As you exhale, envision you whole body relaxing. You can also meditate on Scriptures like **With God all things are possible** (Matthew 19:26) and envisioning your stressful situation resolving miraculously.

***

2.

Abdominal Breathing

Abdominal breathing or deep breathing is one fastest ways of counteracting the body's stress response. It is done by inhaling through your nose until your abdomen rises, holding your breath for a few moments and then exhaling completely through your mouth until your abdomen collapses. This cycle of filling the lungs with air, pausing and then emptying them can be repeated for 15 minutes every day.

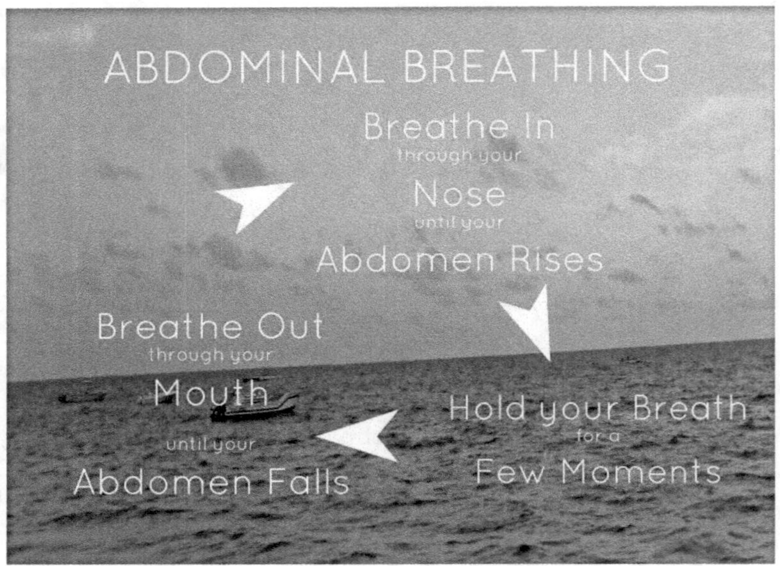

***

3.

Guided Imagery

Guided imagery is another effective relaxation technique. It involves visualizing yourself in a relaxing environment. Therefore close your eyes, take several deep breaths and use your mind's eye to see yourself relaxing on a beach or floating on a cloud or walking through a garden or whichever environment makes you feel relaxed. Use all your senses to immerse yourself in the restful environment by seeing soothing images, smelling appealing scents, hearing calming sounds, tasting and feeling your way through it. After you have enjoyed our visit, bring yourself gently back to reality.

***

4.

Problem Solving Visualization

Visualization can also be used to manage stressful situations. To do this see yourself with your mind's eye in your most stressful situation and then envisioning yourself using various strategies to cope. For example you can imagine yourself dealing with a stressful boss by breathing deeply until you no longer feel distressed by their words or actions.

***

5.

Physical Exercise

When a person is stressed, they tense their muscles. Stretching exercises reduce this muscle tension and help a person feel relaxed.

Aerobic exercises help the body burn circulating stress hormones that contribute to the development of stress related illnesses.

Weight bearing exercises also aid in stress management since they demand concentration and help a person forget their problems.

Therefore engage in regular physical exercises to manage stress.

****

Relaxing Activities

Other relaxing activities that you can engage in to manage stress include:

1. Journaling since writing down uncensored feelings is a very effective method of catharsis. It is doubly effective when combined with writing lists of things you are thankful for.

2. Listening to calming music.

3. Engaging in hobbies that complement their main job

4. Helping less fortunate members of your society like visiting the sick in hospitals since this takes your mind off your problems

5. Drinking soothing herbal teas like chamomile and passionflower.

6. Eating foods which raise serotonin levels like turkey, salmon, chicken, cheese, chocolate, wholegrain bread.

7. Watching comedy since laughter relieves tension.

8. Spending time with your social support system.

****

Stress Management Plan

Stress Management Plan Week 1

Day 1

1. Abdominal breathing

2. Meditation

3. Physical Exercise

4. Watching Comedy

Day 2

1. Abdominal breathing

2. Meditation

3. Drinking herbal teas and eating serotonin rich foods

4. Watching Comedy

Day 3

1. Abdominal breathing

2. Meditation

3. Physical Exercise

4. Watching Comedy

Day 4

1. Abdominal breathing

2. Meditation

3. Drinking herbal teas and eating serotonin rich foods

4. Watching Comedy

Day 5

1. Abdominal breathing

2. Meditation

3. Physical Exercise

4. Watching Comedy

Day 6 and 7

1. Abdominal breathing 2. Meditation 3. Spending time with your social support system

Stress Management Plan Week 2

Day 1

1. Abdominal breathing

2. Guided imagery

3. Physical Exercise

4. Listening to Music

Day 2

1. Abdominal breathing

2. Guided imagery

3. Drinking herbal teas and eating serotonin rich foods

4. Listening to Music

Day 3

1. Abdominal breathing

2. Guided imagery

3. Physical Exercise

4. Listening to Music

Day 4

1. Abdominal breathing

2. Guided imagery

3. Drinking herbal teas and eating serotonin rich foods

4. Listening to Music

Day 5

1. Abdominal breathing

2. Guided imagery

3. Physical Exercise

4. Listening to Music

Day 6 and 7

1. Abdominal breathing 2. Guided imagery 3. Engaging in Complementary Hobbies

Stress Management Plan Week 3

Day 1

1. Abdominal breathing

2. Problem solving visualization

3. Physical Exercise

4. Journaling and writing gratitude lists

Day 2

1. Abdominal breathing

2. Problem solving visualization

3. Drinking herbal teas and eating serotonin rich foods

4. Journaling and writing gratitude lists

Day 3

1. Abdominal breathing

2. Problem Solving Visualization

3. Physical Exercise

4. Journaling and writing gratitude lists

Day 4

1. Abdominal breathing

2. Problem Solving Visualization

3. Drinking herbal teas and eating serotonin rich foods

4. Journaling and writing gratitude lists

Day 5

1. Abdominal breathing

2. Problem Solving Visualization

3. Physical Exercise

4. Journaling and writing gratitude lists

Day 6 and 7

1. Abdominal breathing 2. Problem Solving Visualization 3. Helping the less fortunate

Stress Management Plan Week 4

Day 1

1. Abdominal breathing

2. Meditation or Guided Imagery or Problem Solving Visualization (choose the one that has been most relaxing for you and practice it regularly)

3. Physical exercise

4. Watching Comedy or Listening to Music or Journaling and writing gratitude lists (choose the one that has been most relaxing for you and practice it regularly)

Day 2

1. Abdominal breathing

2. Meditation or Guided Imagery or Problem Solving Visualization (choose the one that has been most relaxing for you and practice it regularly)

3. Drinking herbal teas and eating serotonin rich foods

4. Watching Comedy or Listening to Music or Journaling and writing gratitude lists (choose the one that has been most relaxing for you and practice it regularly)

Day 3

1. Abdominal breathing

2. Meditation or Guided Imagery or Problem Solving Visualization (choose the one that has been most relaxing for you and practice it regularly)

3. Physical exercise

4. Watching Comedy or Listening to Music or Journaling and writing gratitude lists (choose the one that has been most relaxing for you and practice it regularly)

Day 4

1. Abdominal breathing

2. Meditation or Guided Imagery or Problem Solving Visualization (choose the one that has been most relaxing for you and practice it regularly)

3. Drinking herbal teas and eating serotonin rich foods

4. Watching Comedy or Listening to Music or Journaling and writing gratitude lists (choose the one that has been most relaxing for you and practice it regularly)

Day 5

1. Abdominal breathing

2. Meditation or Guided Imagery or Problem Solving Visualization (choose the one that has been most relaxing for you and practice it regularly)

3. Physical exercise

4. Watching Comedy or Listening to Music or Journaling and writing gratitude lists (choose the one that has been most relaxing for you and practice it regularly)

Day 6 and 7

1. Abdominal breathing

2. Meditation or Guided Imagery or Problem Solving Visualization (choose the one that has been most relaxing for you and practice it regularly)

3. Spending time with your social support system or Engaging in complementary hobbies or Helping the less fortunate (choose the one that has been most relaxing for you and practice it regularly)

ABOUT THE AUTHOR

Dr. Miriam Kinai is a medical doctor and freelance health writer/blogger.

You can visit her blog at http://www.MyBlogBookClub.com or follow her on twitter at http://twitter.com/AlmasiHealth

Email enquiries to almasihealthcare@yahoo.com with BOOKS as your subject.

HERBS AND SPICES FOR THE COOK, HEALER AND BEAUTICIAN

Herbs and Spices for the Cook, Healer and Beautician uses color pictures and clear explanations to teach you about more than 70 healing herbs and spices.

You will learn about their:

* Therapeutic (healing) uses

* Drug interactions

* Contraindications (when not to use them)

* Cooking tips

* Beauty tips

*****

INTERNATIONAL GOURMET HERB AND SPICE BLENDS

International Gourmet Herb and Spice Blends teaches you how to prepare exotic herb and spice blends from around the world. You will discover the recipes for:

* Barbecue Rub, Cajun, Apple Pie and Pumpkin Pie Spice Mixes from America

* Pudding Spice Mix from Britain

* 5 Spice Mix from China

* Berbere Spice Mix from Ethiopia

* Curry Powder and Garam Masala from India

* Bouquet Garni, Herbs de Provence and Quatre Epices from France

* Herb Mix from Italy

* Jerk Seasoning from Jamaica

* Shichimi Togarashi from Japan

* Pilau Spice Blend from Kenya

* Chili Powder from Mexico

* Baharat Spice Blend from the Middle East

* Ras El Hanout from Morocco

*****

THE QUICK GOURMET CHEF

The Quick Gourmet is an essential culinary skills cookbook which teaches how to make simple, divine dishes.

You will learn how to make:

* Hot Chocolate Mixes and Drinks

* Hot Chai Tea Mixes and Drinks

* Hot Coffee Mixes and Drinks

* Sensational Smoothies

* Non-Dairy Smoothies

* Chocolate Covered Strawberries

* Chocolate Truffles

* Healthy Chicken Salads

* Healthy Tuna Salads

* Savory Salsas

* Herb Butter

* Cheese Dips and Sauces

* Gourmet Sandwiches

* Perfect Hard Boiled Eggs

* A Cheese Board

* Natural Food Color

*****

HOW TO STYLE AND PHOTOGRAPH FOOD

Regardless of whether you are an aspiring food blogger or you want to make money online selling stock photos, How To Style and Photograph Food, uses color pictures and clear explanations to teach you the food photography tips that can help you improve your digital camera photography skills so that you can begin photographing food like a pro.

You will learn:

* The equipment that you need

* How to set up the lighting

* How to prepare the stage

* How to style the food

* How to shoot the food

*****

HOW TO MAKE NATURAL SKIN CARE PRODUCTS VOLUME 1

How To Make Natural Skin Care Products Volume 1 by Dr Miriam Kinai is filled with recipes for making organic bath and body products for normal, sensitive, oily and dry skin types as well as therapeutic products to manage mature skin, prematurely aging skin, cellulite, eczema, psoriasis, ringworms, dandruff, thinning hair, menopausal symptoms, pre-menstrual tension (PMS), painful periods, arthritis, stress, sadness or depression, mental exhaustion and insomnia.

This book also teaches you the best vegetable oils, essential oils, natural butters and herbs to use when making products for different skin types physical conditions. You will learn how to make:

* Bath bombs

* Bath melts

* Bath salts

* Bath teas

* Body butters

* Body lotions

* Body scrubs

* Healing balms and body creams

* Herb infused oils

* Natural soap

How to Make Natural Skin Care Products Volume 1 will leave you with a clear understanding of how to make bath and beauty products to use in your home or to give as gifts or to sell and make money.

*****

ORGANIC SKIN CARE PRODUCT INGREDIENTS

Organic Skin Care Product Ingredients teaches you about the different natural substances that can be used to create natural bath and beauty products to use in your home or to give as gifts to your loved ones or to sell and make money.

You will learn about:

* Natural butters

* Natural clays

* Natural colorants

* Natural exfoliants

* Natural fragrances

* Natural oils

* Natural preservatives

*****

THE ESSENTIALS OF AROMATHERAPY ESSENTIAL OILS

The Essentials of Aromatherapy Essential Oils by Dr Miriam Kinai teaches you how to use aromatherapy oils to improve your physical, mental and emotional well being.

The author's experience as a medical doctor and clinical aromatherapy practitioner have enabled her to write a highly informative guide for those who want to utilize the healing benefits of these natural plant essences.

You will discover:

* The safety information and therapeutic uses of 18 essential oils

* How to blend essential oils

* The characteristics and uses of 14 carrier oils

* How to Dilute Essential Oils with Carrier Oils

* How to Use Essential Oils

* Cautionary Measures when using Essential Oils

* Numerous Essential Oil Recipes for bath products as well as skin care and hair care products

The Essentials of Aromatherapy Essential Oils will leave you with a clear understanding of how you can safely use aromatherapy essential oils to heal yourself naturally.

*****

CARRIER OILS GUIDE

Carrier Oils Guide teaches you the characteristics, health benefits and uses of commonly used carrier oils. You will learn about:

* Apricot Kernel Oil

* Avocado Oil

* Borage Seed Oil

* Calendula Oil

* Carrot Seed Oil

* Castor Oil

* Evening Primrose Oil

* Fractionated Coconut Oil

* Jojoba

* Olive Oil

* Rosehip Oil

* Sunflower Oil

* Sweet Almond Oil

* Virgin Coconut Oil

* Useful formulas for Diluting Essential Oils with Carrier Oils

*****

MEDICAL AROMATHERAPY FOR HEALTH PROFESSIONALS

Medical Aromatherapy for Healthcare Professionals by Dr Miriam Kinai teaches you how to use essential oils to treat physical diseases and emotional disorders.

The author's experience as a medical doctor and clinical aromatherapy practitioner have enabled her to write a highly informative guide for those who want to utilize the healing benefits of these natural plant essences.

You will discover how to use essential oils to:

* Treat skin diseases like acne, eczema and psoriasis

* Treat other physical diseases like high blood pressure, arthritis, coughs and colds

* Manage mental and emotional conditions like anxiety, depression, anger and stress

* Relieve the symptoms of menopause and premenstrual tension

* Lessen insomnia and impotence

Medical Aromatherapy for Healthcare Professionals is therefore an essential resource for holistic healthcare practitioners like massage therapists, naturopaths and herbalists.

It is also a useful resource for conventional medicine healthcare providers like physicians and nurses who want to begin practicing integrative medicine and for patients who want to improve their health naturally by using aromatherapy oils.

*****

AROMATHERAPY COURSE

Aromatherapy Course by Dr Miriam Kinai tutors you on how to use essential oils to improve your physical, mental and emotional well being.

The author's experience as a medical doctor and clinical aromatherapy practitioner have enabled her to create a highly informative course on how to use these natural plant essences.

You will learn:

* The safety information and therapeutic uses of essential oils like clary sage, eucalyptus, geranium, grapefruit, lavender, lemon, lemongrass, marjoram, orange (sweet), patchouli, peppermint, Roman chamomile, rose, rosemary, sandalwood, spearmint, tea tree and ylang ylang.

* The safety information and therapeutic uses of carrier oils like apricot kernel oil, avocado oil, borage seed oil, calendula oil, carrot seed oil, castor oil, evening primrose oil, fractionated coconut oil, jojoba, olive oil, rosehip oil, sunflower oil, sweet almond oil and virgin coconut oil.

* How to blend essential oils

* How to dilute essential oils with carrier oils

* How to administer essential oils

* How to make natural healing products from numerous aromatherapy recipes

* How to utilize the healing benefits of essentials oils even if you do not have prior training in aromatherapy

The Aromatherapy Course will leave you with a clear understanding of how you can heal yourself and your family naturally by using essentials oils on your body and in your home.

*****

DEALING WITH DEPRESSION NATURALLY

Dealing with Depression Naturally presents a holistic approach to managing depression with natural antidepressants. You will learn how to treat depression with:

* Aromatherapy

* Art therapy

* Christian Biblical principles

* Chromotherapy

* Diet therapy

* Eco-therapy

* Herbal therapy

* Home decor therapy

* Music therapy

* Phototherapy

* Exercise therapy

* Self-Psychotherapy

* Social therapy

* Talk therapy

* Vitamin therapy

* Writing therapy

*****

CHRISTIAN LIFE COACHING HANDBOOK

Christian Life Coaching Handbook offers a Biblical approach to managing different aspects of life.

You will learn:

* Christian anger management

* Christian conflict resolution

* Christian depression treatment

* Christian goal setting

* Christian marital stress management

* Christian stress management

* How to assert yourself

* How to defeat fear

* How to love yourself

* How to overcome shyness

* How to resist temptation

* How to stop being a people pleaser

*****

CHRISTIAN PERSONAL FINANCE

Christian Personal Finance teaches Biblical principles of money management.

You will learn:

* Christian financial stress management from people who were dealing with money stress like the Acts 3 beggar or credit issues like the widow in second Kings.

* Biblical prosperity principles from wealthy men and women of God like Isaac and the Proverbs 31 woman.

* Bible verses to use as **spiritual warfare prayers** and as Christian finance affirmations and Christian money meditations.

****

ANTHOLOGY OF CHRISTIAN BIBLE SERMONS

Anthology of Christian Bible Sermons is a compilation of more than 20 Biblical rhema teachings which include:

* A New Christmas Message

* A New Easter Message

* Are You A Flamboyant Fig Tree Christian?

* Biblical Lessons for Purim from Queen Esther

* Can God Help Me If I Am Surrounded By Enemies?

* How Badly Do You Really Want It?

* Seed Words And The Powerful Tongue

* Spiritual AIDS

* The Three Levels Of Getting Lost

* Why Does God Allow Suffering?

* Your Life Is Your Ministry And Your Storm Is Your Message

* A Perfect God, Imperfect People, and Perfect Plans

* We Are Not Ignorant of His Devices

* How to Prepare for a Dangerous Journey

* Yes, God Can

* How to Serve the Body of Christ

* Conduits of God

* Go Back? Stand Still? Move Forward? Drown?

*****

CHRISTIAN SPIRITUAL WARFARE

Christian Spiritual Warfare teaches you the awesome Bible verses you can use as spiritual warfare prayers, Christian affirmations and in your Christian meditation sessions as you fight your spiritual battles.

You will learn how to fight for the following with Bible verses:

* Marriage * Children * Health

* Christian Faith * Christian Ministry

* Country

* Finances * Job * Business

* Peace of Mind * Restoration * Self Esteem * Self Love

You will also learn how to fight against the following with Bible verses:

* Addiction * Temptation

* Being Single * Infertility

* Opposition * Oppression

* Worry * Fear

* Feelings of Condemnation * Confusion

* Danger * Death * Despair * Discouragement

* Impatience * Insomnia * Laziness * Loneliness

* Poverty * Pride * Sadness

* Vengeance * Weakness

* A Foul Mouth * Lying

*****

DARK SKIN DERMATOLOGY COLOR ATLAS

Dark Skin Dermatology Color Atlas is filled with clear explanations and color photos of skin, hair, and nail diseases affecting people with skin of color or Fitzpatrick skin types IV, V, and VI.

Topics covered include Acne Vulgaris, Alopecia Areata, Anal Warts, Angioedema, Aphthous Ulcers, Atopic Dermatitis, Blastomycosis, Blister Beetle Dermatitis or Nairobi Fly Dermatitis, Cellulitis, Chronic Ulcers, Confetti Hypopigmentation, Cutaneous T Cell Lymphoma, Cutaneous Tuberculosis, Dermatitis Artefacta, Erythema Nodosum,

Exfoliative Erythroderma, Gianotti Crosti Syndrome, Hand Dermatitis, Hemangioma, Herpes Zoster, Ichthyosis, Ingrown Toenails, Irritant Contact Dermatitis, Kaposi Sarcoma, Keloids, Keratoderma Blenorrhagica, Klippel Trenaunay Weber Syndrome, Leishmaniasis, Leprosy, Leukonychia, Lichen Nitidus, Lichen Planus,

Lichenoid Drug Eruption, Linear Epidermal Nevus, Linear IgA Dermatosis (LAD), Lipodermatosclerosis, Lymphangioma Circumscriptum, Miliaria, Molluscum Contagiosum, Neurofibromatosis, Nickel Dermatitis, Onychomadesis, Onychomycosis, Palmoplantar Eccrine Hidradenitis, Papular Pruritic Eruption (PPE), Paronychia, Pellagra, Pemphigus Foliaceous,

Pemphigus Vulgaris, Piebaldism, Pityriasis Rosea, Pityriasis Rubra Pilaris, Plantar Hyperkeratosis, Plantar Warts, Poikiloderma, Postinflammatory Hyperpigmentation and Hypopigmentation, Post Topical Steroids Hypopigmentation, Psoriasis, Pyogenic Granuloma or Lobular Capillary Hemangioma, Scabies, Seborrheic Dermatitis, Steven Johnson Syndrome (SJS) and Toxic Epidermal Necrolysis (TEN),

Sunburn, Systemic Sclerosis, Tinea Capitis, Tinea Pedis, Tinea Versicolor, Traction Alopecia, Urticaria, Vasculitis, Vitiligo, and Xanthelasma.

*****